MAC,
The Story of a Pimp

MAC,
The Story of a Pimp

A MEMOIR BY

JAMES McGOWAN

ISBN: 979-8-90252-125-9   (Paperback)
ISBN: 979-8-90252-126-6   (eBook)

Printed in the United States of America

I am James McGowan, aka Jmac. I was born just outside of Memphis in a little small town called Somerville Tennessee. My mother and father had to leave this small rural farming town just East of Memphis about forty miles away. They moved to Memphis when I was a few months old. My father was a farmer and a part time bootlegger. When he got to town he had a suitcase full of alcohol with him and not a lot of money. My mom was run out of town, because she was something of an activist. I believe that she stole the The County Ballot Box and cut the sheriff with a knife. There was a lot of illegal voting activity, going on in the south. It was the Jim Crow era. The sheriff said"you got to be out of town by sun down". So that's where we started. At least where we started on my moms side of the family. My dad's father was a white man who raped my grandmother at the well in 1941. Her name was Grandma Lucy. Lucy Watkins. The matriarch of our family. Try getting a conviction in Tennessee during Jim Crow. And they did try to get him legally but they couldn't. He even raped her a second time and she had another son my dad's brother. So they had to accept the fact nothing was going to be done. I didn't grow up knowing my father's side of the family, the white side of the family. I only grew up knowing my mother's side of the family. I would ask my father about his father but the subject was taboo. When they moved to Memphis, I went to school at Gordon and Grant Elementary. I was one of the first kids to be integrated in the Memphis City School System. Five of us were sent to an all white school called Gordon Elementary in Smokey City where I lived. Those were some of the most trying years of my young life. We were always fighting the white kids. Getting sent home meant a butt whipping. Mom didn't play that. I grew up there. I went to Humes Junior High School where Elvis Presley also went to high school. I left there. I went to Northside High School. Graduated from Northside High School in 1971. I believe the number one picture that year was Super Fly, The Mack was my favorite. Everyone wanted to be a Pimp or Hustler. I grew up a black kid living in one of the poorest neighborhoods in North Memphis. My mother and father made sure we had everything we needed. I had no other source of income. I grew up in a shot gun house. My mother and father tried hard to buy a house. They never seem to be able to buy a house or a car in the early seventies and the late sixties. They were not able to. Colored people, as we were called were poor. The inflation rate was rampant. I graduated from Northside High in 1971. My father was a sanitation worker. When Dr King came to Memphis it was personal. My father, RIP Mr.John McGowan, my sister Charlene McGowan RIP and I were in the march for civil rights.

My father was a city sanitation worker at the time. I was in that parade at 14 years old. When Dr Martin Luther King was killed, all of the kids in our neighborhood ran the five plus miles to downtown Memphis. It was absolute chaos. We hastily made Molotov cocktails. The whole city was burning, on fire. Rioting,marches, looting. It wasn't just downtown Memphis but the whole city. Beale Street was hit especially hard. I mean we ran all the way downtown. We didn't wait on the buses. We didn't wait on a ride. If we didn't have one, we rode bikes. That was a really defining day in my life. After that I didn't want to go to college. All I wanted to do was hustle and I did that. I was OG from the old neighborhood. Some things I did at the time I do regret. I regret bringing drugs to the neighborhood. Getting everybody on them. The drugs were not a good thing.I didn't like selling drugs. As soon as I got on my feet, I got me a nice Cadillac. It was a 1967 Sedan Deville in nineteen seventy five,my first car. In six or seven months I graduated to a nicer ride. A smooth nineteen seventy two Cadillac Fleetwood Brougham I bought some nice taylor made three piece suits. Eggleston the Taylor is where all the"Pimps got Taylor made, So a pimp could get Taylor Paid". I always had to get the girls. I stood around 6 ft 3,175 lbs." I'm slim in the waist and handsome in the face". In high school I had two girl friends. Both were fine cheerleaders. I knew then that I was going to be a pimp.

And I'd be the best there is and the best there was and the best there ever will be. After stacking up enough money. I started riding around recruiting. I came up with some really nice females. They all wanted a better way of life. I made sure that they had it. I started off in Memphis Tennessee. I started my girls on a couple new spots in Memphis Brooks, Road and Lamar avenue. Midtown was also good to me. I made a lot of my in that area money. One hundred a day was the tab. That was the Quota for each one of my hookers. We have a club in Memphis called Club Paradise. It's where all the Pimps hang out on Wednesday nights. It was a cold Christmas Holiday, we were all there for the Prince Phillip Mitchell show. Champagne and cocaine and weed was on the menu. In walks Teddy Pendergrass. We were in the back room shooting craps. When he came in, I tried to send a girl to break him. At the time, he was a top entertainer in the music world. He made women scream with his timeless romantic ballads. But alas Teddy P turned out to be gay. It was confirmed when I saw him hugging and kissing Prince Phillip Mitchell. I liked his jewelry. But I had to make a move, I had traps to check. A bitch better have my money. Jmac was my name, Big Pimpin was my game. A young black and up and coming pimp. I was working my hoes in Memphis and I was getting action from a hoe known as Big Linda. She wanted to choose me but I didn't take females that didn't live up to my standards. I mean, if she doesn't look like money, I didn't want her. I liked bitches who could either steal or look so good, that getting money wasn't a problem. Now she was a good hoe, a vet in the game. My roadie, Booni Mack came up with Big Linda. She paid him like a pimp supposed to get paid. The Memphis Police kept me pulled over. I always had nice cars, big boy jewelry, pretty women and nice clothes. I wore a different silk and mohair suit everyday. Once this rogue cop named oncer Reba, pulled me over, told me and my pimp friend Lil Dave to get on the ground. I refused to get down on the ground. He had drawn his pistol by now. Luckily a black police Lieutenant arrived on the scene. I had on a white silk and mohair suit. I wasn't arrested but I got a ticket for GP. It was during the time of our great Mayor W.W. Herrington. He passed a law saying that the City Police could not pull black people over because they were black. He stopped the dreaded u turn pullover. He stopped stereotyping. In those days, I was definitely a clothes junkie. I was "Seven deep with No Sleep". I was getting my money. I quickly outgrew my hometown, Memphis. All my friends were out of town getting money. The next logical move was to go out of town. My hoes and I hit the truck stops on I-40 in Jackson Tennessee, then on to Nashville Tennessee, Murfreesboro Road and Dickinson Road. It was country as hell. I didn't care. I was getting paid. Over the years I would use Nashville as a pit stop to get money. When I lived in Nashville. I did have to put my hands on a pimp. Not a proud moment in my career. But it was very necessary. A Memphis pimp, new to the game. Mack T was his name. He put his hands on one of my girls. There was nothing to discuss reasonably. My guy didn't have to be told that again. There was this small Club in Nashville on 8th Avenue where all the Pimps hung out.They had a stage show that I really liked. Later, I would eventually use this same act at my club. They would have five girls come out to the sound of Brick House. A song by the Lionel Ritchie and the Commodores. They all had top hats. Each girl had a security guard. The security guards then would put the top hats on the floor in front of each girl, two Top hats each. The DJ would then say, all you pimps and players come to the stage! The so-called players and pimps would then bum rush the stage. They were as in strip club talk making it rain. To make it rain, that's when a guy just rains dollars bills on a females body. Pay each female to shake it. Those girls would shake their asses and break those tricks. Those top hats were overflowing with cash. We would shoot a little pool. I won lots of money in that club. I'm pretty good at the pool game. One night during the holiday season at the club, I was just having drinks and kicking the bobos with the guys. In walks a fine, sexy, voluptuous stripper. Kandy was her name. I bought a round of drinks and one thing lead to another. Before too long I added to my stable. Kandy Kane was her name. Pleasing Jmac was now her game. Of course she broke herself.

I left Nashville for DC. I love Washington DC. Its a predominantly black town in this country not run by whites where knives were legal maybe that's why every hooker had one. There were hookers as far as the eyes could see on 14th Street in The District. I mean there were young hoes, old hoes, and fine hoes. I had super fine ladies. I put their asses in Tranc. Now, Jmac had hoes on the track. I got in my brand new Cadillac Fleetwood along with my pimpin friend Lil Dave. By sun up the next day, I had Five thousand dollars I mean that is pretty good for a rookie in the game. Breaking hoes that's what we did. Everything was going smoothly, everything was Rico Sauve. I got paid in the shade. We rode around sweating hoes, slamming Cadillac Fleetwood doors. At the time, I had a 1972 white and black Fleetwood the year was 1975. I was 21 years old, looking good getting paid. "Let the tricks get laid but the pimps get paid". I was a young blood, green in the game. But I didn't listen to everything that came out of a bitch's mouth. "I stayed down for my crown, putting it in from sun up to sundown". Now they say Pimping ain't easy. That's for real. Anybody can come up with a hoe. Can you get a long run out of her. To get paid by a hoe for years. It takes a certain kind of nigga. Even though, my pimp game was strong. My catch game was stronger than just about anybody in the game. In those days pimps were a rare breed. You have to realize that in the 1970s Washington DC was infested with, hookers junkies, robbers and thieves. There were dope dealers and junkies on every corner. There was a different drug on every corner. Whatever you needed you could get for your hookers. That is if you had hookers that were on drugs like most of the pimps in Washington DC. The DC pimps really hated Memphis pimps. My road dog Booni Mac and I would ride to New York to shop. I enjoyed riding over to the Big Apple to buy some jewelry or maybe a new mink coat. Getting money was the easy part. Staying out of the way, staying out of prisons. You have to be careful because as in most cities, Washington DC has some notorious prisons. They have two very large Federal Prisons. There's Little Lowell and, Big Lowell over in Virginia for, just for pimps. You could get five to ten years for transporting hookers across the state line, five to ten for living off the proceeds. If you were stopped while bringing hookers from Virginia to Washington DC or from Maryland to DC. Every now and then they would have a sting on the bridge coming into DC from Virginia. It was to stop pimps with hookers in the car. So we had to get smart. We started sending them in cabs and on Rapid Transit the L train. That didn't help a pimp friend of mine named

Goldie McDowell from Bunker Hills, Memphis. He did time in lil Lorton for pimping and pandering, 10 years. Goldie, RIP. He died in Dallas after getting a kidney transplant. We hung out on 14th Street, anywhere from DuPont Circle and 14th to P or R streets. There were hookers as far as the eyes could see. Memphis, hoes and Pimps had invaded the town by this time. Kandy turned out to be one of my best hoes. She absolutely loved Washington. There was no limit to how much she brought home on any given night. Tricks road in from Virginia, Maryland and all the East coast. They came because it was nearly legal to sell sex in the District of Columbia It was freedom to exercise your constitutional right to get money. After breaking the hoes in your stable, me and the other Memphis Pimps would hang out at the After Hour joints down on P and Q Streets. Killer Joe was the proprietor, the house man. Killer was originally from Memphis but he was DC now for sure. If you keep going down 14th Street you get to Pennsylvania Avenue then you'll be at the White House. If you go the other way to the hood. There's Soul food restaurants on Florida Avenue and 14th. There's Little Saigon on Q and R Streets. Thousands of Vietnamese Refugees, had come to the US. believing they could be a part of the American dream. I believe that they built a Police station there. It's called Gentrification. In those days there was nothing but the junkies and drugs on those four square blocks. And in that surrounding area.

I mean thousands of people 24 hours a day. It reminded me of Jew Town in Chicago. People were just wandering around doing drugs and selling drugs, or anything that you want to buy. From mink coats to gold Rolex watches and diamond rings. Anything that they stole the night before or the previous week.

This is where everyone came to sell it. This was Little Saigon. It was 1976, 1977 and the Vietnam War was going on. Drugs were being smuggled into the city in body bags. Through the local mortician, who was one of the biggest drug lords of the time, anliated with Frank Lucas. Those were the good old days. In those days I was a young black man doing whatever I could to get by. They were drafting black men into the Army. To go overseas and fight in Vietnam. We didn't have any rights here in America. We didn't know what tomorrow or the next day might bring. I was draft eligible. Soon my number would come up. It hadn't yet. The draft wasn't random. They did it alphabetically. I Thank God for President Nixon ending the war with Vietnam. DC was great for me. We sometimes would ride over to New York City on the weekends. If we were lucky enough to score some tickets, we would catch a Knicks game. Sometimes after l work, Me and the girls would get a bite to eat at Sylvia's in Harlem. We would go to Baltimore Maryland during the week. Maybe, I'd buy some gator shoes at the Gator Shoe Store. Just have a good time. The parties, every night. After a few years I had to get out of DC for a while. We traveled the entire East Coast during the seventies and eighties. Next up was Boston. I loved it. I got money in Boston on Kneeland St Downtown. I mean thousands and thousands. I had so much money stacked away in Boston. I would send Western Unions to myself in other cities before I arrived. The commute in Boston was brutal. Having to drive the Tobin Street toll bridge two times a day. The view from that bridge is breathtaking. Ships in Boston harbor look as if they were toys. This particular winter had been an extremely long and brutal winter in Boston. I had two dressers full of money. I decided to spend my birthday in DC. It was on my birthday. I can't remember exactly which birthday. I had a new hooker her name was Vickie Davis. And she was a thief. I got her in Memphis Tennessee during the Christmas Holidays. She was working in Midtown. I hit her with "Big Hoes Making Big Hoe Moves, Ain't no Confusion in the Choosing She walked over to my car she got in my car. She said Ooh, I like your style. I choose you, she said. I said bitch you ain't gave me no money. Where your money at? She said pull over right here. We had only gone a few hundred feet. I pulled over. There was a very voluptuous white chick working the block right there at that time. You have to understand, that the lesbian hookers were working Midtown Memphis at the time. Long story short, she picked her pocket while playing with her pussy. Understand she did this right there on the spot. She then jumped her fine ass back in the Caddy, she said here Daddy as she gave me what turned out to be six hundred dollars. It's just a down payment she said. I'm thinking good hoe, roguish, klepto my favorite kind. All about the Hog Killin. It was a good day. She gave me what is none as a choosing fee. When a girl gets with you she has to have some money. She can't come to you broke because you can't serve her pimp unless she's paid you. Otherwise, you violated the game. So to keep the game straight and keep my Macn and pimpin and cool and my rep straight. I tried to serve her man. The last man that she was with. He was somewhere out of town. I never got a chance to serve Leroy Townsend. Vickie was a Vet. You pimp by all the rules with a Vet. I kept it pimpin all the time. I did have a family member that lived in Washington DC. Once while there this guy came into my room. I was in the shower. When I came out, he was just standing there holding my jewelry. I caught him trying to steal my gold jewelry. I leaped over the bed to position myself between him and the only way out. And that would be over my dead body. He had around eighty thousand dollars in jewelry in his junkie hands. That a bar room brawl ensued is an understatement. I kicked some junkie ass. My girl arrived and called the police. I got tired of holding him down. He ran and jumped over the rail, he ran off limping. He threatened to get me. That's not the only time that God was with me. I mean only God could get someone out of that kind of trouble. There was another incident in Milwaukee, Wisconsin. I was looking at 50 to life in prison for pimping. They wanted to send me Jmac where they sent Iceberg Slim. Waupan State Prison is somewhere in rural Wisconsin. They don't play around. They hate blacks. They hate Spanish people. They love to tag and stereotype Spanish men as rapists. Black men are labeled as robbers and murderers in Wisconsin. So be careful if you go to Wisconsin. They will railroad you. I spent a year and a half in jail in Wisconsin. I broke this bitch when I first got to Wisconsin. I had a brand new Park Avenue. An 80 Park Avenue it was 1981. I just bought it in Memphis. Silver beautiful car, with red crush velvet seats and interior. I was cruising the blvd one night. I saw this hooker run out of a Downtown Milwaukee hotel. She ran down the alley like it was an emergency. When I saw that look, naturally I got thieves, so I knew one when I saw one. She had just stolen something. I picked her up knowing that she was going to get in because she was trying to get away. She said she liked my style. We kicked it for a while, stayed out all night. Hanging out, like she was mine. I was shooting my shot at this fine bitch.

After going to the after hours spot, we were having a ball drinking cognac, and snorting cocaine. Then I broke her. I knew she had the money in her tits. I didn't have to touch her. She reached me the money. Then the bitch said it was Fifty Six hundred dollars. She said, Jmac please can I have at least a thousand to take home. She said that her man was going to kill her.

I can't go with you, she said. You know that I got babies at the house,she said. I'm a cold hearted pimp. Having ice in my veins I responded, you get nothing from me hoe. That's what you get for playing with a Pimp, I said. At that very moment the police who are always cruising the lake and patrolling, were there at the lake. It was six am. It was morning, sunrise. After being out all night, we were still a lil high. Lake Michigan, that is where everybody came to in the morning. The police cruised by and she panicked and jumped out. She started running and screaming. I would not give her any of the money back. She started screaming that I raped her and I robbed her. At the last second I had to think of something fast. I threw the money out of the car behind her. I tossed my pistol out on the side of the hill. It was wet outside. It had rained that morning at the lake. It landed about twenty feet away. The cops asked me if I wanted to give a statement. I told them that she tried to rob me. They asked me about

                    JAMES MCGOWAN

the pistol that was found in the grass. I said I don't know anything about a pistol in the grass. They took me to jail. They took her to give a statement. I was booked, locked up and detained in the Milwaukee County jail. I had to file a Discovery Writ while I was in jail. I did this in order to see what they had. Suspiciously my court appointed attorney wasn't telling me anything. He was trying to help them railroad me. He was appointed by the court, so naturally he's getting paid by the state. He gets paid not to win against the state. His name was Mark Peterson he was my duly Court appointed legal council. He never told me about the finger print evidence. Or lack there of. There were no prints on the gun. It had rained. Again I took what I read in Helter Skelter. I used it. You can't get fingerprints on a wet weapon. It also requires at least ten points of similarities. They hid the evidence of her having been on her cycle that night. There was no evidence of blood or DNA. None was found in my car or on me. They swabbed her throat and mouth, nothing! Everything came back negative. But instead of dropping the case, they would try Railroading me. While I was in jail, I did meet some Muslim brothers. They put me up on the game. I was told that in Milwaukee, the local establishment loves sending black men to prison. They have a known practice of Railroading black men. My Muslim brothers said, Memphis don't forget to take your Bible with you when you go to court. They called me Memphis during the time I was locked down in Milwaukee. Another Muslim brother said, Memphis be sure to watch your back when dealing with those Devils. They will lie then try to deceive you, if you are not careful. Be watchful the Muslim brother said. He repeated it, as if to put an exclamation point on it. They love to put black men in jail in Milwaukee for things that they haven't done. They will railroad you in a second if you aren't careful. Watch everything that they do. Those were extremely prophetic words. When I did go to court my lawyer did the worst. The time came to select a jury of my peers. My duly court appointed PD, attorney wanted to allow a retired police detective on the jury. The ex detective had been on the force for 30 years. He wanted him on the jury. I mean of course he did. He was purposely trying to help sell me out. The ex detective was asked if he knew anybody who still worked at the Milwaukee sheriff once or Police department. That he had been retired for 7 years. Well of course after 30 years of service he still knew some people in the dept. That surely had to be a lie. If you are going to allow him on my jury. I definitely don't want you defending me. I had been informed that the charges carried a maximum penalty of Fifty years to Life in the Waupan State Prison. There's a part of the trial called the VoirDire phase. phase. That's where you and your attorney get a chance to remove three people from the jury pool. If indeed you want to or you just don't like them. He didn't want to remove him. He completely ignored me. I knew then he was actively trying to help railroad me. He said that a detective would absolutely know the truth when he heard it. That we should leave him on the jury. I said there's no way. There were two things that I learned when I got to Milwaukee County Jail.

As there were two books in my cell when I got there. One book was the Bible. The other was Helter Skelter by Charles Manson. I read them both. So I did employ the same strategy that evil Charles Manson employed in the murders, written about in Helter Skelter. I fired my attorney in front of the jury and in front of the judge. The angry and obviously frustrated judge wanted to lock me up in the back. He said you can have a trial by video. Before he could do it I stood up. In front of the Jury, I yelled out. I don't want him. He's not representing me correctly. He's not my attorney. I don't want him representing me. I said he doesn't have my best interest at heart. The judge was pissed. He said sit down Mr Warrington. I didn't give them my real name when I got arrested. I can't for the life of me understand it. Why didn't they make me claim my real name. Especially when I was sworn in. I was under an Alias. The Judge said Mr. Warrington sat down. You can't have a new attorney. I said, Your Honor this man is not competent, he is not representing me correctly nor competently. At that stage, the Judge told the deputy to escort the jury out. They were returned to the jury room. He told me I would be taken out and handcuffed. I would have a video trial, if I didn't sit and cooperate. I read about that maneuver in the Charles Manson book. I was totally prepared for it. I said that I understood. I had no choice but to act as if I was playing along. As soon as he bang his gavel and reopened the court, the deputy brought in the jury. At that point I stood up again. I said, I reiterate Your Honor this is not my attorney. He doesn't represent me. The judge lost it and went off. This devil was working really hard. He asked the jury whether they were prejudiced by my outburst. They all said resoundingly yes. They were indeed prejudiced. They all felt I wasn't getting a fair trial. The prosecutor was very hot by this time. That meant the state of Wisconsin, which had already spent millions of dollars on this trial. They would now have to spend millions more. To give me a new trial was going to be costly. The law says that I was entitled to a fair trial. I filed a motion firing that court appointed sell out attorney, Mark Peterson. They had to declare a mistrial and appoint me another attorney. Not a court PD but independent council. And they gave me the best attorney in the state of Wisconsin. His name was

Thomas Halloran. He drove a white Rolls-Royce. He had an once in the tallest building in downtown Milwaukee Wisconsin. Now I had real representation. He was as I said, an excellent attorney. When it became time to either retry me again or not. They made the decision to retry me. They didn't make that decision lightly. Now is where it really gets critical. They set my return court date a year later. A year later I walked into the Milwaukee County Courthouse. Only this time I won, a unanimous acquittal. I was in such a hurry to get out of that place, they called Milwaukee. I didn't worry about all the clothes they had taken. I didn't worry about the car they had taken. I know that I did perjure myself by giving a false name under oath.

In hindsight, I should have sued them. All I wanted was that fifty six hundred and to leave Milwaukee. I wanted the money, yea I wanted it. It was the principle of it all. I had gone through so much for it. I had given a whole year of my life for what, peanuts. When I first arrived in Milwaukee I had five hookers with me, Three broke bad. They left at the first sign of trouble. One my favorites Cindy B testified at my first trial. She was convicted of perjury. They sent her out of state rather than give her five years for perjury. She got five years probation and a floater out of town.

She went down trying to lie and get me off. The other one was my bottom girl. KK She stayed on and helped me beat the case as a witness for the defense.

She obtained Milwaukee ID. She got a job as if she was a hard working female from there. She testified at the trial, and I won my acquittal due largely to her testimony. So it was no wonder I loved her. She was the one, she was the best. Later I found out that, yes they did indeed repossess my car. They didn't take it for pimping. They did take all my suits. All of my clothes. The reality was that I had to start over. No problem, I've done that before.

Nora J was her real name, we called her slim or Karen Johnson, KK. She was the best. Nora was a very special person. She was My Bottom, my right hand. She was not a flat backer. She was a real money getter. We got money doing some not so legal or legit things. She did a seven year bit in the Alderson, West Virginia Women's Penitentiary. It was for Fraud. She could play the secretary role. Just a little con and grifting to supplement the income. Nora was full of life and love, fibrant with a light that seemed to shine through even on the stormiest of days. She had this joy about her, a sweetness. She was my backbone and I was hers. She was and always will be, the love of my life. Let me speak on the way I got into the game. She turned me out to pimping in real life. It was not some shit you see in a movie like the Mack, Sweetback or SuperFly. If a bitch ever hurts you by crossing you for money. And they are going to hurt you. Put your feelings in your back pocket. Turn it around, don't block the money. Make sure you get paid. Get the dollar bills y'all, the Mulah, the Denaro. The way I first met Nora,she was also my first. I was hustling,gambling and selling weed in The Bay area of my home town. The Greenbrier Apartments is where I was living with my baby mama. I was hustling out of her place. I had a nice Cadillac. I was getting my props right, so that I could come up with a hooker. I needed a hooker to finance my dream of getting rich, pimping. That's when I met Her, KK, aka Nora J, she was kicking it with two other bitches. They all were roommates and stayed in one apartment. They all had niggas they fucked with. I came through we kicked it, she didn't belong or represent anybody else. It was written in stone. We got together. Everything was going well. Until one night she got out of pocket. I left the apartment. When I got back an hour later she wasn't there. She went out. At that time she had two kids previously. I was with the kids all night when she came in at five in the morning. She didn't have any money. No money. Now I wasn't a pimp at the time. But I know that shit wasn't working. That was the making of a pimp. If you give your heart to a bitch who at that time didn't deserve it and you're green you don't know any better. When a bitch does something foul, breaks your heart, you going pimping. Or you can be a trick ass nigga and get hurt over and over. "From ashes to ashes and dust to dust, show me a woman you can trust". Circumstances can change your life. They will make you go pimpin real fast. That way you get paid. You don't get hurt. So Stay Pimpin, Stay Pippin young nigga. Get your game straight, keep your name straight and your pimping will always be great. I made plenty of money in Memphis to start my Pimp career. Old school tracks, like Vance ave, Mulberry st, Midtown, McLemore and Mississippi is where I started out. I opened my own track, Lamar Avenue, and Brooks Road. I was the originator of these two spots. I had beef with a South Memphis pimp by the name of Lil Moose. We had a shootout on Lamar in Nineteen seventy Five it was a territorial dispute. I had the stroll, hoe track whatever you want to call it. I didn't plan on sharing it. Actually it was hoe shit and I always say, let hoes deal with hoe shit. But he didn't see it that way. After he shot up my car, I pulled out my Baby, a jet Black Colt Commander 45 caliber and that was the end of that. Later on in life, Lil moose and I would have another run in. But that's later on in this story. At the time I was seven deep with no sleep. I had five black girls and two white girls. All my white hoes at that time worked out of cars in Midtown Memphis. If you had a white hoe she had to have a car. If you wanted to maximize your money. I was all about maximizing my money. It was around Spring of 1979. I had just arrived back in Memphis for the holidays. I had a new son, 9 months old. I went to see my son and his mother. Upon unlocking the door and walking inside the apartment, the apartment that I paid for, and had a key to. I was in for a big surprise. Standing with what looked like a 25 automatic, my gun in his hands, one I left for home protection. A man, I've never seen before. I immediately drew my gun, he shot and I shot. He went down, He was extremely lucky I wasn't shooting to kill. He tried to shoot me, but he missed. I didn't miss him. He was hit in the right side, hip area. The police arrested me as I was making my getaway. An Action News 5 helicopter 8 police cars, firefighters and EMTs all greeted me as I attempted to flee the scene. I was arrested and both guns were found in my car. After making bail. I fought the case for 2 years. I made a deal with my son's mom. She would move to Atlanta and not testify against me in court. I was offered twenty years but I didn't take it. They got desperate and offered me ten years. The Prosecution couldn't understand why I wouldn't accept the ten years. They rearrested me for attempting to bribe a witness. They couldn't prove that charge. I had a rabbit up my sleeve. No witness no case. The guy I shot, had a heroin charge in Chicago. That case was still pending. He now had a warrant out of Chicago. He missed a court date. They offered me one last offer. It was for 5 years. I didn't take the deal. The City of Memphis would eventually have to completely dismiss the case Without Prejudice. That means that I couldn't be charged with the same crime again.

Memphis had left such a bad taste in my mouth. That's when I decided it was time to make a move, after all the drama. It really needed to be somewhere out of town, close. Logically that meant somewhere like Nashville or the Big Easy, New Orleans. At that time I really didn't know how to stay away from the dope game. I would buy a fifty five pound bail of marijuana in New Orleans. It only takes around six hours to bring it back to Memphis. I would flip it. Then send my hookers by airplane to different cities. I stacked my money two ways. At that time I didn't know how not to mix two games. My nigga, a real gangster from South Memphis named Big Ike, He lived, well it was a trap house in the projects called known as Clayborn Homes. He and I would ride to New Orleans maybe every two months. Where I'd hook him up with the Italians. He would buy a fifty five pound bail of weed. I usually made six thousand per trip. It was during one of those trips that Ike and a couple of his guys went to New Orleans without me. Needless to say that it didn't end well for them. One thing about Italians, they don't trust anybody or anyone. And you show up without an appointment, unannounced and without the hookup. I can imagine they became very leary, suspicious. Well my guys were robbed. One was shot in a sugar cane field and died, his son was critically wounded, while my friend Big Ike was traced back the hotel. They found a hotel room key on his dead friend. Police found Big at the hotel with thirty two thousand in cash, the killers got away with over twenty eight thousand dollars. Most of which was found on the killers when they were apprehended. Needless to say, I haven't been back to New Orleans since that incident. Basically, that would signal the end of my drug selling career. I decided to make another move back to my home state of Tennessee. I moved to Nashville. I lived in a little suburban town outside of Nashville. The town of Antioch Tennessee was actually where my family's slave roots originated in this country. I stacked a bank, saved money working Murfreesboro Road and Dickerson Road. Nashville is unique it has a metropolitan style government, the same as New York City. That's extremely beneficial to pimps. Any misdemeanor has a set Bond. Meaning, you don't have to go to court after bailing out. The fine is the Bond. I was making preparations before I left for Florida. Soon after arriving in Miami, I immediately realized that South Florida was Paradise for a Pimp. In the upcoming weeks Miami would be hosting the Super Bowl. The city would have to host thousands of tourists. Some were coming soon. I was there thirty days ahead of kickoff time. The hotels and motels were all booked solid. The early bird catches the worm. Every year I was in Miami or New Orleans at least a month before the Super bowl. During the earlier Superbowl years it was either of the two cities. Each of my girls had quotas of five hundred dollars each. Now this was in the early nineteen seventies. That was a lot of money at that time. I was clocking anywhere from Three thousand dollars to five thousand dollars every night leading up to the Super Bowl. Thats not to mention all the gold chains, diamond rings, Rolex rings Rolex watches and cocaine that your girls could bring home. Living in Miami you can believe bitches brought dope home every day. Miami is my second favorite city. Sunny weather, breeze beaches, perfect for whatever you want to do. If it's jet ski, or water polo, swimming, renting a forty feet Yacht for a party on board or just relaxing on the beach in a chaisse chair. It was just par for the course. Even when they didn't originally do drugs. In those days we all tried different things. Some girls did pills. We hung out at the Wreck Bar on South Beach, 163 & Collins Blvd. It was a half sunken wrecked luxury yacht that was creatively converted into a nightclub. I was having cocktails at the Wreck Bar. That's when my girl

JAMES MCGOWAN

Slim called me one night from a cell phone, at the time I didn't recognize the name or number. Cell phones had just came out. The phone was of the brick variety, it came with its own case. She was somewhere inside the Gated Community off of Biscayne Boulevard. Now Biscayne Boulevard is the hoe stroll in Miami. But it also has entrances to the luxurious multi million dollar estates and mansions on Biscayne Bay.She wanted to know what to do. She had robbed a trick and knocked him out with knockout drops. She had a lot of money and a lot of jewelry. She didn't know how to get out of the gate. I instructed her to locate the car keys and drive out. I also told her not to roll down the window. Be calm and drive out the very same way. Are the windows tinted I asked? She said that they were. I asked if Security had rang them in. She said yes but that they hadn't spoken to the guard in the shack. The security guards are usually lazy and dozing off around that time of the night. The gate should open up automatically and let you out. When she came to the security shack no one could see who was in the car. If they tried, the tint on the windows are called limo tint for a reason you get complete privacy. The gate swung opened and let her out without any problem. They didn't stop the limo. As instructed she parked the limousine about a mile and a half from our apartment. I left the Wreck Bar and I drove North on the 79th street Causeway.

I drove to meet her. After arriving at the rendezvous spot,I picked her up.She had a small cloth bag stuffed with gold jewelry. It was one of those old Crown Royal liquor bags. Without the alcohol of course. There were three nice Rolex watches. A Presidential Rolex watch solid gold, a Submariner Rolex watch stainless steel and gold, and a smaller ladies Rolex, four big gold chains. All in all it was about Seventy five thousand dollars in jewelry. There was also Ten thousand in cash. Those were known as the Disco days. During that time we were all sniꝴng, blow or powder. People got high on the dance floor at all the cool discos. They had sex in the club. Sometimes right on the dance floor. So I knew that the heat was on after the theft. We stayed inside for a week, until the heat cooled off for a minute. The police were hot .I had to make a move. You see, anytime anyone that's important gets taken for a ride in Miami, there are real consequences and or repercussions. Later that night, we crept out of town. We stopped in Orlando Florida. My partner Lil David, was powdering his nose at the Churches chicken on Orange Blossom Trail of all places, right.Of course he was seen by an undercover oꝴcer. She was a beautiful undercover oꝴcer I must say. The next morning we would awaken in the Orange County Jail. We were fingerprinted and booked for the quarter ounce of powder. It was around seven grams. That was in the late nineteen seventies. Everyone around the world snorted powder cocaine. The seven grams were luckily all that we had on us. Of course we'd skip town the next day. A few hours later we arrived in Washington DC. I hadn't seen that many hookers since Biscayne Boulevard in Miami during the early seventies. But I, Jmac was standing there looking at the city that was going to make me rich. I had finally made it back to Washington DC.There were hookers everywhere from the White House, to the Hoe house. Pennsylvania avenue and 14th all the way down 14th Street to O, P, Q, R, S to Florida Ave. Every alphabet you can think of. On every last one of those streets were drugs. There are different drugs on every street. On P Street they had heroin. On O Street they had pills. They also had different pills on different streets. In those days it was Bi62 meth pills. Preludin in Memphis cost twenty dollars per pill but in Washington DC they only cost five dollars. So a lot of guys would spend hoe money to buy dope or pills. They would bring it back to Memphis. They would flip it. I still had the dope game in my blood. So when I first got there, I did that a couple of times. "But ain't no money better than HOE money". I was trying to get all the money. I mean I was clocking dollars. I mean I had thieves and I was pimping, I was getting so much money it was scary sometimes. I had five fine hookers at the time and they were all getting paid. Nora Aka Karen Johnson, Cindy

B AKa Mary Massey, Stacy, Sharon V, and Vickie Duncan. She's not to be confused with the most roguish, klepto in my career Vickie Davis, RIP.I was on a return trip to DC where a trick tried to rob one of my hookers on my birthday. $$$$ Vickie D. had stolen a twenty thousand dollar gold and diamond pendant chain and eleven thousand dollars in cash on my birthday. That was her birthday present to me. She called and said, Baby I can't get home fast enough with this for you, she said before hanging up the phone. Before she made it to me, she got way laid by a robber. She called me and said she didn't want to lead him to the motel room. So when she told me she was at the once. I hurriedly raced to the once. With that kind of money on the line I wasn't taking any chances. I had on a silk two piece and it was late at night or in the early morning hours. I went to the once and out of nowhere this guy hit me in the head with a bottle. Vickie was screaming at the top of her lungs.After he hit me in the head with the bottle, she had her knife open trying to cut him. I pulled out my knife, and with one swipe I cut his guts out. As he ran across the street towards a paddy wagon, I said stop him. I didn't want him to die. He was holding his guts in his hands at that point. A Police Paddy wagon was at the donut shop. We were on New York Avenue and Bladensburg Parkway.

                                    JAMES MCGOWAN

He ran towards the police. I felt like I had two heads. My head was swollen, so bad and I couldn't think straight. The only thing I could think of was to get away. I felt like he was going to die. I had blood all over me. I ripped my silk shirt off and threw my clothes in the garbage bin. I sent her to the hotel room to pack the bags. She packed really fast. We got the hell out of there. There are taxis all over the place in DC, all night long. It takes all of three minutes to get a taxi anywhere in DC.

It's always crowded even though the EMTs were taking care of him across the street. I felt he was going to die. I didn't want a murder charge in DC. We were in a direct line with the Baltimore Parkway. We went straight to the airport. We did, it was maybe twenty five miles in the taxi. We quickly caught a red eye flight to Memphis. I was in Memphis for maybe three or four months before the FBI, the Memphis Police, Sheriff deputies and the Federal Marshall, all showed up at my Mom's door. I was wanted in Washington DC on charges, Flight to avoid prosecution, Assault with Great Bodily Harm, attempted murder, all because of a cut throat nigga. To this day I don't know if he passed or what. Got arrested at my mom's house. They tricked me out of the house with the ruse that a car had run into my car outside. So naturally my car is a Cadillac. I ran outside to my shock and amazement.

I went to jail from there, then I got turned over to the feds and I went to court. I went before the judge the very next day. The Federal Prosecutor turned out to be my ex lawyer Tim Dizsenza. What a rare coincidence. Arch Boyd my present attorney took his place at the law firm. The law firm I started out with. My attorney Arch Boyd who would also become a dear personal friend. We went into that Federal Courtroom with a friend as the opposing council. On the way to court, we just happened to get on the elevator with Tim Diszenza the newly appointed Federal Prosecutor. He spoke to Arch. Then he asked if there was anything he could do. Arch said no, at which time I responded with a resounding YES! We all had a good laugh. Once we were in the courtroom, I received an OR, or Own Recognizance Bond. That was unheard of. My court date was set for February 17, a significant date because it's always snowing in DC at that time of the year. There was a blizzard the day before we left and during the drive up with my partner Red Lester. We had one lane to drive on a three lane freeway. We took interstate forty over to interstate sixty six. I could only follow closely behind Semi trucks that were only doing 35 mph. I could only see 2 car lengths in this blinding blizzard. But I had court and it was the 16th of February. We finally arrived around 1am. We slept in the car till morning. Went to my estranged cousin's for breakfast.

I got the surprise of my life when I realized, my cousin was a Gay Pimp. My things have changed. I couldn't eat, but Red Les had no problem eating, he demolished some chicken wings. After he had his fill and I said my good byes. I went to court. God kept me again. Facing a judge with my freedom at stake. I didn't go to court unprepared. I had a great defense. I asked to speak with a detective on the case. I explained the guy I cut was the same guy who tried to rob me months earlier. I caught him in my room with my jewelry in his hands. I had to fight for my life in that motel room. I subdued the thief, held him for twenty minutes. I pinned him to the floor. I couldn't hold him any longer. Dude was high on Sherm. I couldn't hold him any longer. I started getting tired. I released him. He escaped by jumping over the second floor railing like a ninja and limping away. He said he was going to get me. That he would be back. The case was Dismissed!!!! But God. Except for a couple of episodes Washington DC was absolutely great to me. Legal U turns made my job easy. I mean coming up with new girls, sweating other pimps girls, looking for the Choosing. Big hoes making Big hoe moves. Hookers do choose. They choose to get in a better situation, a better man, a new life, new daddy, wife inlaws. All this goes with Pimpin.It ain't easy cause now they got several drugs your girls can get on really quick. Then the dope man got her, and she is virtually his. While in DC we would ride over to BMo, Baltimore MD, when we hit the dope spot, they were always playing Memphis on their boom box.8 Ball and MJG. Memphis is recognized world wide. After securing the weed or whatever, we'd ride through downtown Baltimore MD. Most shopping days I would purchase four maybe five pairs of new Alligator shoes. A gator two piece suit to go with my New David Eatons. After leaving, Baltimore. We headed north on the New Jersey turnpike to New York City. I needed to buy some fresh jewelry to keep my fronts up. Maybe a fresh mink coat. Minks coats are cheap in the Big Apple. Diamonds are really affordable. You get a lot more for your money. You are dealing with the source, no middle man. Life is also cheap in New York, so if you know who, what, and where is a good thing. At the time my homie from my hood in Smokey City, Eddie Adair Aka Godfather was a big man in Harlem. He ran some shit. Had the Jamaican Posse gang. We would ride through and score from one of his bodegas. That's a store with very little on the shelves. Its a front for selling drugs. We would shoot a little pool and hang out in Harlem. Stop and get some soul food, at my favorite place to eat, Sylvia's Soul Food Restaurant in Harlem. I worked the big Apple with Kandy Kane, but there was so much money being made uptown. I had my other hoes drive up. I love to work the girls in one city and I would hangout in another. So I would ride to Boston Massachusetts. Bean town as it's called is a great town. We got plenty of money and hardly any problems with the law. You could get a run in as long as your hookers weren't stealing. It was hard for me cause I would hit town and everything is going well. The girls are getting paid, but hoes have very competitive spirits. They are always trying to out do one another. This was on a daily basis. Then one of them would steal a wallet full of money, or a Rolex watch. Then it's let's ride or try to work around the heat from the cops. If something was stolen it became extremely hot with cops. A robbery charge is a very expensive charge. It's not a guarantee to get off on the charges.

So, I could either put her on a plane to Atlantic City or Las Vegas. I would stay and check my traps long distance. Western Unions arrived on a daily. I lived just outside Boston in Lowell Massachusetts. After, three years burning up the city of Boston Massachusetts.

We left for Montreal Canada. Within a month, I knocked a sweet French Mademoiselle in Montreal. It only lasted 6 months. She couldn't speak very much English. We made it work.

It was a good idea to take French in school. Everyone spoke French in Montreal. It was like being overseas.

It was like being in Paris France. The architecture, the buildings are amazing Toronto is another story, at least you could get a real meal. Its a three hour drive north on the kings highway from Detroit Michigan, Toronto is a beautiful city, Jamaican food is the closest thing to Soul food. Oxtails, Jerked chicken. I finally got back stateside, as they say. I couldn't wait to get a real meal for myself. And neither could my girls. Bitches had lost weight in Canada. We had to come back home. We needed some American food. When we did come back. We came through the Midwest. I stopped and got money in Michigan. I love Grand Rapids Michigan.

I met Denise, aka Deni in Grand Rapids Michigan. She was a young and beautiful snow bunny with blonde hair, blue eyes, and the future mother of two of my kids. At that time she was a young hooker with some guy out of Chicago. She was looking for a new home. So KK brought her home. She wanted to choose my pimping, but with no money. That was a problem easily solved. I got her ass back out on that track. She had to get my money. The choosing fee. Told her, Let your next choice be your best choice. That she chose Memphis'best. She stayed for a few months. After around six months, she did brake badly. That means she didn't't come home, she didn't return to the sender. I didn't have any time to spend with her. I was

　　　　　JAMES MCGOWAN

"Five deep with no sleep". "Purse First Ass Last", is what I lived by. So a couple weeks later she brought her ass back to a Real Pimp. After arriving at my next stop in Cincinnati, I made a boat load of money. Just on the other side of the bridge in downtown Cincinnati is Newport Kentucky. What looked ok for just one night, turned out that it wasn't. We got three rooms, One for me and my nigga and two for the hoes to rest. We had a trip to Memphis scheduled for the next morning,so I thought. I was fast asleep when I got a call from the girls. It's three am. They were informing me that some tricks were next door to them. They had beer and wanted to party. How did they know that you were there I asked? She said that she was going to the ice machine, when she was approached by him. I told her, Vickie don't. Go to bed! The next thing I know cops are barging in the room arresting us. The charges were for Pimpin, Living off the Proceeds. We all spent a whole year in jail eating barley soup and bologna sandwiches. One sandwich per meal and a bowl of barley water. My lawyer flew in to try and get me out. But he was told all they wanted was the ten thousand dollars I had on me and the four thousand dollars my partner Lil Dave had. Now there were 10 of us in a jail that was recently condemned,only to reopen just to house us pimps and hoes illegally. The town of NewPort Kentucky, a Mob town with Commonwealth laws. That means they can change a law basically whenever they want. Overnight if necessary. When I didn't cooperate, they put our trial off for a year. I could see my car from the jail window and it was snowing in the spring when we first arrived and it was late Spring the next year when they took us to court. Thirteen months later. They took my money and Lil Dave's, they did let us go with enough to get home. But I didn't go to Memphis, like I should have. I went to Milwaukee Wisconsin. As soon as I arrived, I knocked a female that I saw rob a trick. She ran out of the rear door of a hotel in the downtown area of Milwaukee. She jumped into my car. We kicked it all night. We were drinking and partying. We were getting high, snorting blow. I told her to break herself. She said that she couldn't choose me because of her children and the baby's daddy. She told me she wanted some of the money to take home. I didn't see it the same way at all. After you partying with me all night drinking, snorting coke all on me. Now that it was time for her to go, she wanted some of the money back. I said hell no, that's what you get for playing with Pimping.We were on the lake, everyone goes there at sunrise. The cops happened to be passing on patrol. That's when things took a turn for the worse. As they rode past.She jumped out the car, screaming that I had just raped her.That I took her money.Just as she was getting out I had to come up with something quickly. I threw the money out behind her on the ground by the

   JAMES MCGOWAN

door. I told them that she had just tried to rob me. They arrested me for sexual assault and robbery. Fifty to Life is what I was facing. They took me to Milwaukee county jail, I was fingerprinted and locked up. I wasn't a weak pimp. I ran the block in a week. I was locked down. I knew I had to get outta there. I went to court and they tried to railroad me off the bat. My court appointed attorney tried to let a recently retired police detective, remain on my jury. When I first came into the cell, there were two books. The Bible, and Helter Skelter by CharlesManson. I must confess, I read the book by Charles Manson first for some reason. That book prepared me for all the tricks on railroading someone. And they really did try hard. For instance, after firing my attorney in front of the jury like Charles Manson did. I did get a mistrial. I was then appointed the best attorney in Wisconsin, Thomas J Haloran. I had a retrial and won a unanimous decision. I shook every jurors hand. I retrieved the fifty six hundred I had broken the bitch for. I didn't even go for my belongings, I just wanted out. Cindy B went down swinging. They gave her a floater out of town. She tried her best to give me an alibi. Thinking to myself, I got to track her down. She thought I had gotten fifty years. But years later I found out from her sister that I had met miraculously at UT. Her sister, Ms Betty Massey said she waited for me for years. You see, after she got the floater out of town,

Milwaukee. She unbeknownst to me, moved back to Memphis. I never saw her alive again, as sadly she passed away waiting on me. Mary E Massey, RIP. Karen, Aka, Nora testified and helped me beat the case. After it was over we left on the first Greyhound. I couldn't believe I'd jumped out of the frying pan into the fire. Was it bad luck? A curse maybe.The bank had repossessed my brand new car. Every suit, every pair of shoes, photos. Everything was gone. All of my clothes were gone. Lost was a mink coat, twenty tailored suits, 5 pair alligator shoes. Starting over was nothing new to me. When I did get to Memphis in the spring of 1982, this young turnout named Sharon V. Sharon was cool with a new face and there was money to be made. I needed something to get high on. My guy had a big bag at the time. Lil Dave and I went to the Plug, Big Ike. We found him at his spot in the Clayborn Homes projects. He pulled out a tray of powder and what looked like crystal. My intro to freebase, crack as it is called now. My guy lil Dave over indulged in what he thought was cocaine. It was actually Angel dust. He would very nearly be O.D. It turned out to be a really bad decision. Now when I lived in Miami I did a lot of powder. Big Ike said this is now the new thing. Free Base. They call it crack now. If only I knew about this form of cocaine before trying it. It was not a social drug, but a serious addiction. I would never have tried it had I known what came with the addiction. Back in Memphis I came up with a hooker named Linda and her friend Giselle. I hung around the Greyhound station in Memphis to knock off potential prospects for my stable. This is where I got them. Around the six months there's a knock on my door at the hotel that we were at in downtown Memphis. Upon opening the door, I'm confronted by to very large and intimidating men with dark hair and wearing suits. The smaller of the two, stepped closer as if to enter but I stood there steadfast. He said we are here for Giselle Gambino. Linda and Giselle luckily weren't there. He explained that she ran away from New York with a black girl, a friend. She was a Mob Princess. They were working at a strip club in Midtown, I chimed. I never heard from either of them again. I decided to go to Dallas, Texas. Harry Hines Blvd is the track, the stroll. Dallas is really nice. I love Dallas. I will never forget that day in Dallas on Harry Hines and Northwest Highway. This white hippie junkie ran in front of my car. I shouldn't call him a junkie. He was headed towards the drug spot. I was headed to another drug spot, I can't throw stones.He ran across the street in front of my car. I couldn't help but hit him. The two cars on my right blocked those two lanes. The concrete curb on my left prevented me from avoiding him. He died in my arms. It was ruled a suicide by automobile. The other drivers stopped and told the cops what happened. I left Dallas after three years. I couldn't stay after that. I went to Phoenix Arizona, as I crossed the state line into Arizona, Deni the blue eyed blonde bombshell tells me she is going to have another kid. After just having my son Demetrius. I was mad asf. I was still roasting her and a nosey ass white woman heard me saying shit, so you know that nosey bitch called the cops. When they showed up, we were at a service station just inside the Arizona state line at a service station. Deni cussed their asses out. And we continued on to Phoenix Arizona. I decided to name my unborn child, ARIZONA.

Phoenix, Arizona and the blazing hot desert sun was infested with red ants, black scorpions, giant tarantulas, sand, and cacti. Phoenix is less than six hours from Los Angeles. We worked on a strip called Van Buren. The desert was more than 110° in the daytime too hot for any bitch. Hoes would work all night long to avoid that heat. And the heat that came with not getting any money. There were quite a lot of Los Angeles hookers up and down Van Buren Blvd. Drag Queens also worked the strip. It was becoming virtually impossible to distinguish a Queen from a woman out there. A lot of them came from LA. They had spent thousands on plastic surgery and were as I said quite indistinguishable. My girls were taking care of a pimps business. I decided to go to the Bay area for a few weeks. So, I hit I-5 north. In eight hours I drove to San Francisco. It was a really smooth ride up. Of course we smoked a little weed and stopped for zuzus. In my brand new candy apple red Cadillac Fleetwood with crushed velvet Interior. I pulled up on Geary and Mission Ave in downtown San Francisco All eyes were on the fly ride. I pulled into the parking lot of the hotel. Travelodge Hotel and Bar is what the neon sign said. The valet evidently accustomed to and familiar with my kind, took my car keys and the twenty dollar tip. He got in the car did a pimp lean and made the tires squeal just a bit, before he disappeared around the corner. I got a room on the 8th floor. I got my girls rooms. I split the crew. I required four rooms around the corner. Then my girls got busy getting my money. Hookers love San Francisco, it's legal. And this for all the young pimps. NEVER LAY YO HEAD WHERE YOU GET YO BREAD. Three days later I added to my stable. I knocked off this Samoan chick. She was from the American Samoan islands. Thats not far from Hawaii. She said she didn't have a man, later I found out she had lied. She chose me with twenty five hundred dollars. Now I'm enjoying Frisco at this point. There was a knock on my hotel room door. I opened the door. Standing there were two big,white guys in suits with badges. They quickly identified themselves as police detectives. We are here about a reported kidnapping. The kidnapping reportedly had taken place earlier in week. He said, put your hands behind your back. You are under arrest. At that very moment my girl Shayna came out of the shower. They started to ask her a million questions, what is going on? She asked anxiously. He asked her, after pulling her to the side. Was she ok? She got loud and that's when she stated with a resolve that made me proud I am here by Choice, not By force she exclaimed. The detectives were bought and paid for by her ex, Philmore Slim, the biggest pimp on the West coast. But my game was strong. I said if that's all you gentlemen need. We have a Warriors Game to attend. Now that's not usually the way it's done. I stayed in the town for a month or two. I didn't get a chance to serve Philmore Slim. He avoided me serving him. That's so he could claim he didn't get served by a pimp. I mean some pimps, especially the older Vets know the game. Who got more action at a hoe than that hoes ex pimp. Unless he was a gorilla pimp. The ones that say "To keep a hoe you have to Beat a hoe". That's not pimping. If you don't get served, that's still your hoe, by technicality only.

After not getting the chance or pleasure of doing so. I took that money getter on tour. She was getting paid the big bucks twenty five hundred dollars to four thousand dollars a day. Budda heads is what we call the Asian chicks. If I only knew what was to come. We toured the entire Northwest, Las Vegas, Reno back down to Phoenix Arizona. One month in everything was smooth as silk. Now this chic was young but, not illegal. A trick who turned out to be a cop, had been dating her. He started liking my girl. Now he felt he had to bust the Pimp. Who better to get info on a Memphis pimp than another Memphis pimp. Lil Moose, still holding a beef, told them whatever they wanted to know. Where to find me, everything. I was locked up for pimping and living off the proceeds. My Bond was set at $100,000. When I got to court, I found out that I had a warrant out of Memphis. It was for armed robbery. It happened when I was in Memphis for the holidays. One of my youngest girls Vickie Duncan, got robbed by one of the twins. I knew them personally. They usually hung out at The Rack. It was a pool hall on Lamar Ave in Memphis. When I asked her what happened, she said twin robbed her of two hundred and fifty. My guy and I rode the blade until we found him at the dope spot. I pistol whipped his thieving ass. He gave me most of the money back. He said Jmac I didn't know it was yo hoe. I said nigga please. I popped a round off into the ground and he ran like a mother. I mean that nigga was high. He was so high that he ran through some tall, thick holly bushes. We all know how that went. Weak nigga, told the police that I robbed him. I shot at him and he was cut up pretty badly from the thorns. He told the cops at the ER, that I robbed him. I decided to not fight extradition and return to Memphis to face charges.

The Memphis charges over-ruled the pimping charges. The charges were dropped and Federal Marshall transported me by airplane, a Boeing 747. I was placed in handcuffs and shackles that were secured around my waist. I was extradited back to Memphis.Now, when a lollipop pimp goes to jail his girls break bad. The really good hoes representing real pimps know what to do. My girls were already on the track getting my bail money. Which was set at Fifty Six thousand dollars cash. I was in jail for a couple months. When we had all the money. I made bail. I was a gangster before I was a pimp. I reverted back to gangster shit. I had Vickie D to file charges against twins brother for robbery and assault. The other one dropped the charges he had against me. It was to save his brother's ass. God has blessed me. I went to jail in numerous cities, Milwaukee, Orlando, Newport, Phoenix, DC, Los Angeles, Memphis. God opened all those jailhouse doors. I beat all those felony charges. In those days we all snorted cocaine. But when the freebase came out, well that's a different story altogether. I was on it for around five years. I got off in 1989 and was sober for 2 years. I wanted my mom to see her baby son drug free before she died. My mom did see me sober from 1989 until 1992. I lost the most precious person in my life in April of 1992. RIP, My mother Annie L McGowan. She was always saying, what are you going to do when I'm gone? Then I would say Mom please, don't say stuff like that. When she did pass away, it was the worst day of my life. I relapsed for a week after she passed. My three year old son Devron was with me. One night I got really high thinking about my mom. I was at her home after she died. When I looked in the mirror, I saw a demon. I was so high off those drugs. My son Devron looked at me. He said Daddy what's wrong? An innocent child saw the demon in me. I said there's nothing wrong son. That was the last time that I've gotten high. I didn't go to a rehabilitation clinic. I did quit. I went cold turkey. That was the last time I've gotten high. I've been drug free ever since. Cold turkey by the grace of God. With a whole lot of prayer. God has brought me out of cocaine addiction. I wish Nora could have quit also. I gave all my girls a choice. I was quitting the cocaine. I asked them if there's anyone else who wants to quit? I said, I will support whatever you decide to do. But Nora J, my heart and soul could not shake it. I felt really bad. I casually introduced her and a number of my girls to snorting powder. Its what everyone did in the eighties. Sometimes she wouldn't come home for weeks. Once, she was missing for quite a while. She was on it pretty badly. My mom liked her tremendously. She worried a lot about her. When she finally came home, my mom passed away. It was not long after. She had worried too much. She also had extremely high blood pressure. Worrying about her and my 14 year old son didn't help. One very unforgettable night, my mother had multiple strokes. Nora rode with her to the hospital in the back of the ambulance. She held her hand the whole way. I followed in my car. She was a beautiful person. That truly was a bitter pill to swallow. RIP, to my mother Annie L McGowan.

In the middle of my misery two of my friends arrived at my mom's house, while I was grieving. They came in from Dallas, Texas. They came to offer their heart felt condolences. Dennis Jones aka DJ and Boonie Mac. Two big pimps pulled up in a big boy S500 Mercedes Benz. I was out of there in the blink of an eye. I was on my way back to Dallas. A place I hadn't been in a while because of what happened before. But I was broke and grieving my mom's death. She had been on life support for two weeks. That was truly a nightmare. The death of my mother took a lot out of me. We prayed for her recovery everyday for two weeks. Having to make the heart breaking decision to turn off my mother's life support. It was hard dealing with the hurt and pain that comes with such a tragic loss. There is no hurt in this world that compares to it. After that, I kept my mind on my business. Nora and I went to Dallas. In a matter of months, I had stacked enough money. I bought myself a new Black Mercedes S500. I came back to Memphis with a pocket full of cash. I took care of the business that I needed to take care of. That included trying to raise my kids. I found a new home and started over fresh. I bought a night club in North Memphis. We called it Club HiRise. I started working my girls in the strip clubs. I wanted to be where I could raise my now, fourteen year old son Devron. It was hectic running a club sixteen hours a day 5 days a week. It was a Rhythm and Blues, Hip hop, night spot.

Wendy was one of my best girls. She made a thousand most nights dancing in the strip club. She wouldn't leave The Queen of Diamonds until she had her money. She never brought in less than $500. I invested in a beautiful new home. We were doing very well. That was until envy reared its ugly head. Her family's interfering ruined mostly everything we built. Wendy had been molested and sexually abused as a child. She was repeatedly raped and abused by her father. She started having mental issues. The older she got the manifestation of things in her past began to take over. I lost a beautiful house with a swimming pool and all the amenities. She started losing her mind. JJs House of Styles was the name of my Barber and Beauty Shop. It would serve as my first attempt at legitimacy. The shop was in the old neighborhood, it was located on Jackson Ave. Thats on the north side of town. It is a really rough side of my hometown. But then, I got the chance to purchase a night club. That was a no brainer. It did very well. It held around four hundred people. Though, I did routinely cheat. We would have five hundred. It was standing room only for a specific act or performing guest or show. That's at least Fifteen thousand dollars in gross proceeds from that night, the Bar proceeds included. Of course, I had to pay for the DJ entertainment, plus five employees. I also bought a couple of condos in the Frayser area. It was then I decided I would try to be a better example for my sons. This was a hard one. The decision to actually change my life and be true to the new person I would become was so difficult. I had my son with me all this time. Sometimes I had to work over night at the club. We had living quarters in the club. My son enjoyed it. I had been in the club business for sixteen years. I felt it was just time to sell. After selling the club, I got a job. Yes, I got a job. I got hired at the University of Tennessee Health Science center. It was a state job with great benefits and pay. I retired from there after 10 years. While I was working at UT, I bought a home for Devron and I. I had been putting money away. I met my grandson Akeem for the first time. He was my son Jamie's son. My son never gave him any love. I felt it was my responsibility to stand in for my son. I spent time, I mean quality time with Akeem. He was sixteen when he came into my life. He was gunned down in a gang related shooting. He was nineteen when he was murdered. RIP, Akeem McGowan. I tried to teach him that if I could change my life around he could. He never got the chance. He was the enforcer for a neighborhood gang. He was marked, set up for assassination by a member of his own crew to be gun down in the cold hard rain. Murdered because of jealousy in regards to a G bitch. Every member was in the train line. His blended partner, had his gun when he was shot. He never returned a shot. At close range no less. I was just devastated. The leader of the gang that killed my grandson lived down the street from my home. As a shy fourteen year old who used to cut my grass, he ordered the hit on my grandson. They were both eighteen or nineteen and he and his friends were afraid of Akeem. The police eventually arrested his friend and the shooter. That's what I was told by my son Jamie, his father. I had street vengeance on my mind. My son didn't and to tell the truth I felt that was not an option. An eye for an eye. I looked everywhere for his friend. He was never at home. He was guilty and he was ducking me. If he wasn't guilty, why run and hide? What about gang retribution? I felt like the cross was involved. I looked everyday for the gang leader. He was no where to be found. So, I sold my house and moved to the other side of town. The plan was simple. The gang members sometimes would play basketball on a street goal directly in front of his house. I'd ride through when he and his friends were hooping, I would exact my revenge. But God did soften my heart. Later when my son gave me the news that they were all arrested.Thank God. During all this I was smart. I paid my taxes. I paid into Social Security. Even though, I was in the streets for thirty years.I made a promise, to retire from the streets at fifty years old. On my 50th birthday I quit the game. The game didn't quit me. It was also around this time, that Nora's life would also tragically come to an end. We were together for a very long time, twenty two years. When the time came we went our own separate ways. It was mutually agreed upon separation. She needed to settle down and get a job. She would have to raise our two children, Tammie and Taurus. One fateful day Nora did drive up to visit our youngest son Devron, who did live with me. It was a dreary, rainy Spring Saturday afternoon when they arrived. It was still drizzling and the streets were wet as she was returning to Oxford Miss. She was trying to get her life in order. She was living with her mom and kids, doing well. Nora had a good job in Mississippi. Tragedy would strike again, God took her home. Before she left my home, I told her to be careful in that little Nissan truck. I had a bad vibe that something was going

                                    JAMES MCGOWAN

to happen. I found out that she had a fatal crash in Oxford Miss. I can never forget it. The pain, but the hardest part was having to tell my sixteen year old son Devron, that his mom was on life support. She had been airlifted from Oxford Miss to Tupelo Miss. You have to understand that's ninety miles from Memphis. Driving that long trip with my teenage son was one of the most difficult things I have ever had to do. After arriving at the hospital, we found her in ICU. We prayed for her, but she was gone. My mom and now, Nora my backbone. This wasn't real, this had to be a nightmare. I was truly grief-stricken, I was devastated. Devron my sixteen year old son strangely held it together better than I did. I do know that it was really hard for him. Tammie, Nora's only daughter my step daughter took care of the funeral and burial arrangements RIP. I was too torn up to be of much help. My beloved Nora J. Mosby. RIP

When I was young, my mother sent us to church every Sunday. Bethlehem Baptist Church it was our neighborhood church. My mother and father never went. I would come home from church, along with my sister. I would then preach the sermon that the Pastor preached to us earlier that morning, to my mother. I did my best. I didn't want her soul to go to hell. She was always saying, boy you gone be a preacher. I missed my calling. I realized later after many years of thinking about it. Sunday was the only day my mom and dad had any privacy. We as kids, my sister Charlene and I were always under foot. I get it now. When I was a young 12 year old I read just about the whole Old Testament Bible. There was always something spiritual in me. All this time, God has kept me. And I truly thank him. I know now that all those cases I beat were by God's, Grace and his Mercy. And not by my own self or own accord. He's still keeping me to this very day. He healed me from stage 4 cancer. I was told that it was the hardest cancer treatment there is. I did lose a tremendous amount of weight during therapy and treatment. I lost in excess of Fifty pounds. Six months of radiation and four months of chemo will do that. God knew my heart. It was he that cured me of Cancer. I know it was him all along, that kept me. I am truly a walking testimony, a real life miracle! God has truly blessed me. Thank you Yahweh, Jehovah Rapha for blessing me in Yeshua's name.Amen

www.ingramcontent.com/pod-product-compliance
Lightning Source LLC
Chambersburg PA
CBHW021811150726
47989CB00004B/1873